![DK] READERS

Level 3

Level 4

A Note to Parents

DK READERS is a compelling program for beginning readers, designed in conjunction with leading literacy experts, including Dr. Linda Gambrell, Professor of Education at Clemson University. Dr. Gambrell has served as President of the National Reading Conference, the College Reading Association, and the International Reading Association.

Beautiful illustrations and superb full-color photographs combine with engaging, easy-to-read stories and informational texts to offer a fresh approach to each subject in the series. Each DK READER is guaranteed to capture a child's interest while developing his or her reading skills, general knowledge, and love of reading.

The five levels of DK READERS are aimed at different reading abilities, enabling you to choose the books that are exactly right for your child:

Pre-level 1: Learning to read
Level 1: Beginning to read
Level 2: Beginning to read alone
Level 3: Reading alone
Level 4: Proficient readers

The "normal" age at which a child begins to read can be anywhere from three to eight years old. Adult participation through the lower levels is very helpful for providing encouragement, discussing storylines, and sounding out unfamiliar words.

No matter which level you select, you can be sure that you are helping your child learn to read, then read to learn!

LONDON, NEW YORK, MUNICH,
MELBOURNE, and DELHI

For DK/BradyGames
Global Strategy Guide Publisher
Mike Degler
Digital and Trade Category Publisher
Brian Saliba
Editor-In-Chief
H. Leigh Davis
Operations Manager
Stacey Beheler
Title Manager
Tim Fitzpatrick
Book Designer
Tim Amrhein
Production Designer
Wil Cruz

For DK Publishing
Publishing Director
Beth Sutinis
Licensing Editor
Nancy Ellwood
Reading Consultant
Linda B. Gambrell, Ph.D.

DK/BradyGAMES

800 East 96th St., 3rd floor

Indianapolis, IN 46240

11 12 13 10 9 8 7 6 5 4 3 2 1

A catalog record for this book is available from the Library of Congress.

ISBN: 978-0-7566-5392-7 (Paperback)

ISBN: 978-0-7566-8700-7 (Hardback)

Printed and bound by Lake Book

Discover more at
www.dk.com

Contents

DK READERS

READING
3
ALONE

Legends of Sinnoh!

Written by Michael Teitelbaum

DK Publishing

What is the Sinnoh Region?

The Pokémon world has many different regions. Each region contains different Pokémon, tournaments, Trainers, Pokémon Gyms, and Pokémon experts. Mt. Coronet, a large mountain, divides Sinnoh. Sinnoh is filled with historical ruins. Some of them are on Mt. Coronet.

Mt. Coronet

These ruins are filled with mystery. Sinnoh also has big cities, such as Jubilife and Hearthome City.

A research center and ruins site in Sinnoh

The Sinnoh region boasts several freshwater lakes. Three major lakes are Lake Verity in the west, Lake Acuity in the north, and Lake Valor in the east. These lakes are important because they are the homes of three Legendary Pokémon: Uxie, Mesprit, and Azelf.

What is a Legendary Pokémon?

Like all the regions of the Pokémon world, the Sinnoh region is filled with myths and legends. Among these are tales of Mythical and Legendary Pokémon. Legendary Pokémon are powerful, special, and hard to find. Very few Pokémon Trainers have ever even seen one.

Unlike many Pokémon, Legendary Pokémon are not known to evolve. Certain Legendary Pokémon seem to have mysterious connections to one another.

Lake Acuity in Sinnoh's northern area

Do Legendary Pokémon come from a parallel world? Do they have the power to control time and space? No one is exactly sure, but these Legendary Pokémon hold a special place for the people of Sinnoh.

The Lake Guardians: Uxie

Three of Sinnoh's Legendary
Pokémon are known as the Lake
Guardians: Uxie, Mesprit, and Azelf.
Each of these

Legendary

Pokémon

observe the

world from

below one of

Sinnoh's lakes.

*Uxie is called "The Being
of Knowledge."*

Legends state that all knowledge came from Uxie. Many believe it was because of Uxie that people suddenly gained knowledge and intelligence. People then used this knowledge to make their lives better.

Like its fellow Lake Guardians, Uxie is believed to have arrived in the Pokémon world long before people even existed. Just as people believe that Uxie has the power to give knowledge, it also has the ability to erase a person's knowledge.

Whenever you see Uxie, its eyes are closed, and that's a good thing! The legends of Sinnoh say that anyone who looks into Uxie's eyes has his or her memory erased!

Uxie rests beneath Lake Acuity. Lake Acuity is in the northern part of Sinnoh, and the weather is often cold.

Brock observes Lake Acuity, believed to be Uxie's home.

Still, those who have ventured up to the frozen north have told stories about a Legendary

Nurse Joy displays a book about the Lake Guardians.

Pokémon floating above the lake. It seems that those who were lucky enough to see this sight caught a glimpse of Uxie.

Examples of Uxie's Moves and Ability

In battle, Uxie uses the Future Sight move. This move is a delayed attack that can take foes by surprise. All of the Lake Guardians move by floating or hovering, using their Levitate Ability.

The Lake Guardians: Mesprit

The next Lake Guardian, Mesprit, is known as "The Being of Emotion." The legends of Sinnoh state that Mesprit taught humans the importance of emotions. Mesprit showed them that all emotions—happiness, sorrow, joy, and pain—are necessary parts of being human.

It is said that Mesprit arrived in the Pokémon world a very long time ago. Mesprit observes the world from below Lake Verity, near Twinleaf Town.

Mesprit is similar in appearance to Uxie, with gems on its double tails and forehead. However, Mesprit's face is pink instead of yellow.

Like its fellow Lake Guardians, Mesprit has great power. People believe its spirit can separate from its body.

This allows Mesprit to fly around Lake Verity.

Mesprit is called "The Being of Emotion."

Dawn and Piplup see a ghostly figure at Lake Verity.

A ghostly figure has sometimes been seen at the Lake. Many believe this to be the spirit of Mesprit. Those who see Mesprit should beware. Never disturb any Legendary Pokémon. In the case of Mesprit, stories say a person who bothers this Lake Guardian can have his or her emotions removed!

In Sinnoh, it is believed that all three of these Lake Guardians may have come from the same Egg. It may also be true that the three are part of the Sinnoh Space-Time legend. This story tells how the Pokémon world was formed. If that legend is true, then Mesprit and its fellow Lake Guardians are very, very old.

Always Aware
Even when Mesprit is sleeping, it can still see what is going on in the world around it.

The Lake Guardians: Azelf

The third Lake Guardian is Azelf, which lives beneath Lake Valor and is known as "The Being of Willpower." It is said that Azelf affects both people and Pokémon, giving them the determination and willpower they need to live their lives. Even when Azelf is sleeping, its great power helps keep balance in the Pokémon world. That alone makes Azelf a very important Pokémon. However, that's just the start.

There's no doubt that Azelf is linked to the other two Lake Guardians.

Azelf is called "The Being of Willpower."

The special connection among Mesprit, Azelf, and Uxie gives them great power. This makes them a target for those who seek to do evil. Many believe that, together, these three Legendary Pokémon can unlock many of Sinnoh's ancient secrets.

Ash and Pikachu view a stone carving resembling Azelf.

Azelf is blue and has three small, red jewels. One stone is on its forehead and two are on its tail. Azelf is a small

Pokémon, but don't let its size fool you. It has great power.

Azelf in battle!

In fact, working together with Mesprit and Uxie, Azelf can calm Dialga and Palkia, two very powerful Legendary Pokémon.

Psychic-types

Like its fellow Lake Guardians, Uxie and Mesprit, Azelf is a Psychic-type Pokémon.

The Legendary Pokémon Dialga

Believe it or not, another trio of Legendary Pokémon is just as powerful and shrouded in legend as the Lake Guardians. The first member of this trio is Dialga, who is known in Sinnoh as the "Ruler of Time."

Dialga

The legends of Sinnoh say that Dialga has the power to control time. These stories say that time itself began moving forward when Dialga was born long ago.

Dialga is one of the largest known Pokémon.

Dialga is 17' 9" tall and weighs 1505.8 pounds. It is dark blue and gray, and it has a huge, blue, diamond-shaped jewel on its chest. Large fins run along its back and head.

The legends
say that Dialga
lives in another

dimension, one that's parallel to our

own. For this reason, people almost

never see Dialga in the wild. Visitors to

the Sinnoh region see statues of Dialga,

but that's about as close to witnessing

this Legendary Pokémon as they get.

Many believe that Dialga controls the

flow of time and can travel through time

at will. Some believe it's even possible to

summon Dialga and Palkia, but to do so

would require immense power.

Since ancient times, Celestic Town in Sinnoh has had a deep connection with Dialga and Palkia. Not surprisingly, there are also ancient ruins in Celestic Town.

The Adamant Orb, now being studied in Celestic Town's historical research center, can make the

The Adamant Orb

already strong Dialga even more powerful.

Roar of Time

Dialga has a special attack called Roar of Time. When Dialga uses the Roar of Time attack, the blue jewel on its chest glows brightly.

The Legendary Pokémon Palkia

Just as the legends of Sinnoh say that Dialga has the power to control time, the ancient tales also speak of Palkia's ability to control space. This Pokémon, known in Sinnoh as the "Ruler of Space," can bend, warp, or distort the very fabric of space itself. Its powerful attack is called "Spacial Rend."

It is believed that Palkia lives in a gap between our dimension and the parallel dimension where Dialga lives.

Palkia can transport itself through space and easily move between these dimensions.

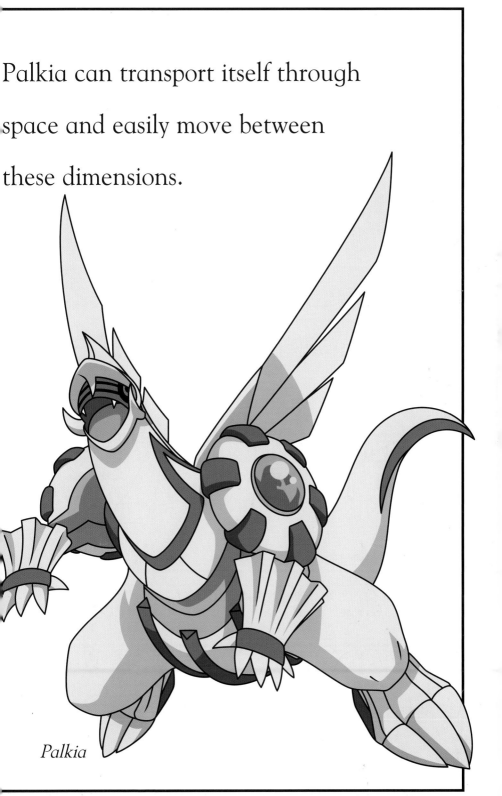

Palkia

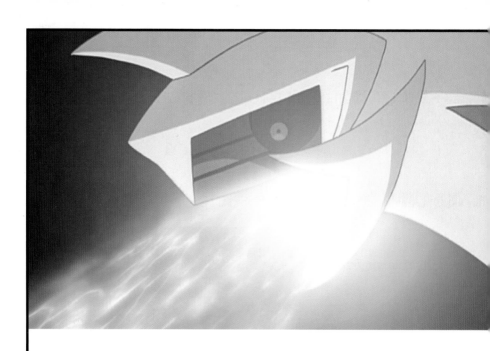

Because Palkia spends much of its time in the space between dimensions, very few people have ever seen it. Even so, Palkia is featured in legends of the Sinnoh region.

Palkia stands 13' 09" tall and weighs 740.8 pounds. An artifact known as the Lustrous Orb makes Palkia more powerful.

The Lustrous Orb

This Orb, like the Adamant Orb, is the subject of much research in Sinnoh.

A Water- and Dragon-type
Like Dialga and Giratina, Palkia is a Dragon-type Pokémon.

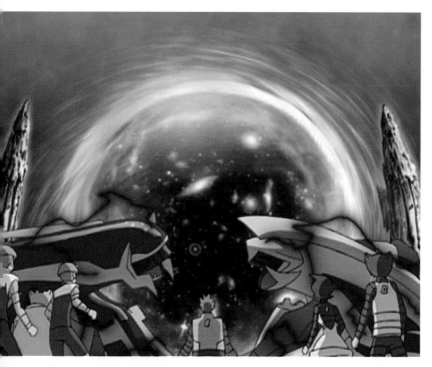

The villain Cyrus summons Dialga and Palkia in Spear Pillar.

The Legendary Pokémon Giratina

    While Dialga can control time and Palkia can warp space, Giratina is an even more unusual Legendary Pokémon.

Giratina's Origin Forme

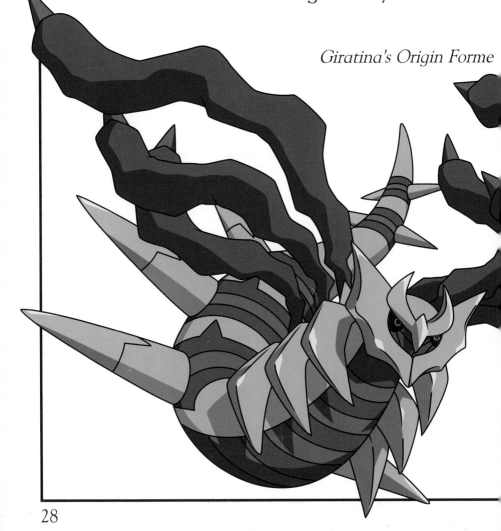

ts very existence is shrouded in mystery. Giratina, the third member of this trio, ives in another dimension known as he Reverse World. Reverse World is a mirror universe, reflecting the normal universe. It is a strange, confusing place where even gravity is different.

Although Giratina is considered one of the Legendary Pokémon of Sinnoh, it is rarely seen in Sinnoh itself. Giratina spends most of its time n the Reverse World.

Giratina can view our world from its home in the Reverse World, and it is the only being that can travel between the Reverse World and our normal universe.

Giratina is one tough-looking Pokémon! In its Altered Forme, it stands 14' 9" tall and weighs 1653.5 pounds. It has jagged wings with sharp horns on them. It also has six legs.

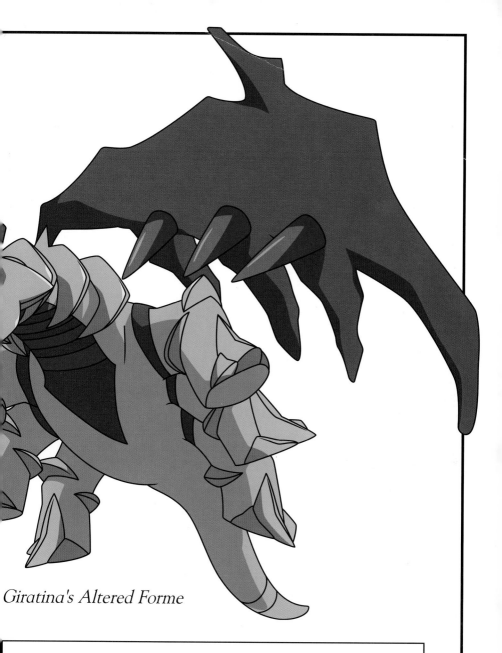

Giratina's Altered Forme

Giratina's Formes

Giratina has two formes: an Origin Forme and an
Altered Forme. It is seen in Origin Forme only in its
own world, the Reverse World. When Giratina is in
the normal world, it is seen only in its Altered Forme.

31

Manaphy

While there are many Water-type Pokémon in the

Manaph

Pokémon universe, none is quite like the Mythical Water-type Pokémon Manaphy. Manaphy travels long distances across the world's oceans in order to find its way back to the bottom of the sea, where it was hatched. That's why it is called the "Migration Pokémon."

Manaphy is tiny. It stands just 1' 0" and weighs only 3.1 pounds. While this Pokémon of the oceans may look tiny and cute, it is truly an amazing Pokémon.

When danger strikes, Manaphy has great power to protect itself and others.

Manaphy hatches possessing a special Heart Swap move, an amazing power to bond with other Pokémon. It uses this power in a number of ways, including sharing its status and strength with others. It can even cause people to swap minds.

All Wet

Because it is such a true Pokémon of the sea, it's not surprising to learn that eighty percent of Manaphy's body is made up of water.

Other Legendary Pokémon of Sinnoh

Regigigas in Snowpoint Temple

Regigigas has a connection to
Regirock, Registeel, and Regice. These
Pokémon have hard, huge bodies. Legend
says that Regigigas, Registeel, Regirock,
and Regice once saved Snowpoint City
from an erupting volcano.

Since then, Regigigas has been asleep within Snowpoint Temple, guarded by the other three Pokémon.

Cresselia is known as the "Lunar Pokémon." Using its Lunar Dance move, it can heal other Pokémon. Darkrai, known as the "Pitch-Black Pokémon," is different. Some say this Legendary Pokémon is connected to darkness.

Cresselia

Its Bad Dreams move gives people nightmares. Cresselia and Darkrai have a strong connection. Cresselia balances out Darkrai's power, easing the nightmares that it brings. Some believe that a Lunar Wing, made from a Cresselia feather, can help keep Darkrai's bad dreams at bay.

Darkrai

Once a year, a Darkrai visits one of the islands that make up Canalave City.

Although it causes nightmares, a Cresselia always comes to drive Darkrai away. Stories say that this Cresselia appears on nearby Fullmoon Island.

Shaymin uses its power to clean the environment. Its Seed Flare move can change toxins that

Shaymin's Land Forme

pollute the air, water, or soil into pure light and clean water. When Shaymin is happy, flowers bloom on its back.

The pollen from a blooming Gracidea flower lets Shaymin transform from Land Forme to Sky Forme. If Shaymin is in its Sky Forme, it reverts to Land Forme at nightfall. Shaymin is also known as The Gratitude Pokémon. When it migrates, people call this migration a "Flower Bearing journey."

Shaymin's Sky Forme

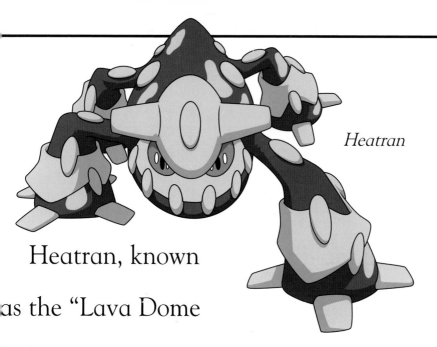

Heatran

Heatran, known as the "Lava Dome Pokémon," was created by fire. Its blood is boiling hot. Heatran digs into the walls of caves formed from volcanic magma and actually lives inside active volcanoes. Its claws help it hang onto the walls of the hot, rocky caverns where it lives. Its Flash Fire power protects it from all Fire-type attacks.

Arceus

Arceus is among the most powerful and mysterious of all of Sinnoh's Legendary Pokémon. According to Sinnoh mythology, Arceus emerged from an Egg and shaped the entire Pokémon world. These myths also claim that Arceus shaped the universe using its 1,000 arms. This Normal-type Pokémon stands 10' 6" tall and weighs 705.5 pounds. It has 16 Life Plates, each possessing a different elemental power.

Arceus

Ash and his Friends Meet Sinnoh's Legendary Pokémon

Very few people have ever seen any of Sinnoh's Legendary Pokémon. Pokémon Trainer Ash Ketchum and his friends Dawn and Brock have been lucky enough to experience several encounters with these mysterious Pokémon!

A Vision of Azelf

One night, when Ash couldn't sleep, he and his Pikachu went for a stroll along the shores of Lake Valor.

Suddenly, the water began to spin like a shining whirlpool. Then

Ash and Pikachu on the night they saw Azelf

something rose from the whirlpool. A ghostly figure appeared. Ash and Pikachu were stunned. They had just seen the spirit of the Lake Guardian, Azelf!

Freeing Cresselia

In Canalave City, Ash and his friends learned that people in town were having nightmares.

Officer Jenny told them that she believed the nightmares were being caused by Darkrai. When Ash, Dawn, and Brock also had nightmares, they headed off to Fullmoon Island to seek Cresselia's help. There, they discovered that Team Rocket had trapped Cresselia in a net. Ash and his friends freed Cresselia, who stopped Darkrai, ending the nightmares in Canalave City.

Saving Shaymin

Another time, Ash, Brock, and Dawn rescued a girl named Marley.

She was protecting a sick Shaymin
that had been exposed to poison gas.
Brock fed the Shaymin a Pecha Berry,
which cured the poison's effects, but
then Team Rocket tried to steal it.
Ash, his friends, and Marley helped free
the Shaymin from Team Rocket and
migrate on its Flower Bearing journey.

Ash, Dawn, Brock, and Marley help a sick Shaymin.

Helping Heatran

When Ash and
his friends found
an injured Pokémon Ranger
named Ben, he explained that he was
chasing a special Heatran. It could use
Eruption, a move that Heatran can't
normally use. He hoped to bring the
Heatran back to the National Park,
but he lost sight of it. Team Rocket had
stolen Ben's Capture Styler and was
also after Heatran. Ash and his friends
helped Pokémon Ranger Ben retrieve his
Capture Styler from Team Rocket.

They also helped him rescue Heatran.
Ben took Heatran to a safe home in the
National Park.

As Ash and his friends have learned,
Legendary Pokémon are an important
part of the Pokémon world. Yet, as
powerful as they are, sometimes these
Pokémon need help from dedicated
Trainers like Ash, Brock, and Dawn.

*Marley's healed Shaymin flies away with other Shaymin
in Sky Forme.*

Glossary

Continent
A huge land mass containing one or more countries

Distort
Change the shape of

Empathetic
Kind, considerate

Gemstones
Colorful, valuable rocks

Magma
Hot, liquid rock that comes out of volcanoes

Parallel
Matching, similar

Region
Area, territory

Shrouded
Covered

Tournament
Contest, competition

Toxin
Poison, pollutant

Vast
Huge

Withstand
Survive, hold up against

Index